Just Trying to Make Sense of It All

To FLORENCE AND VERNON.

ALAN SPENCE

AuthorHouse™
1663 Liberty Drive
Bloomington, IN 47403
www.authorhouse.com
Phone: 1-800-839-8640

© 2012 by Alan Spence. All rights reserved.

No part of this book may be reproduced, stored in a retrieval system, or transmitted by any means without the written permission of the author.

Published by AuthorHouse   03/07/2012

ISBN: 978-1-4678-9036-6 (sc)
ISBN: 978-1-4678-9037-3 (e)

Any people depicted in stock imagery provided by Thinkstock are models, and such images are being used for illustrative purposes only.
Certain stock imagery © Thinkstock.

Because of the dynamic nature of the Internet, any web addresses or links contained in this book may have changed since publication and may no longer be valid. The views expressed in this work are solely those of the author and do not necessarily reflect the views of the publisher, and the publisher hereby disclaims any responsibility for them.

Contents

Preface ix
I wish I was a poet xi

Thoughts About Family Life 1

I tried to write to tell you 2
Suddenly It Just Makes Sense 4
It's time that you both realised 6
I long to be close 8
I need to make it right 10
Bad People 12
Thank heavens for little girls 14
The Parents Lament 16
Responsibility 18
When is it our turn 20
Where are you Jack ? 22
Growing Pains ! 23

What is wrong with the world? 25

Same World Different Rules 26
Just be happy 28
What's it all about 29

Seasonal Thoughts 33

A Christmas Thought 34
Happy New Year 36
So this is Christmas 37

Some thoughts for people I know 41

A Rhyme For No Reason 42
The Magic Man 44
It's Not You 46
Mistakes don't matter 48
You don't know what you've got till it's gone 49

Thoughts about life in general 51

Things to be happy about 52
Choices 54
Tempus Fugit 55
Go back if you need to 56
Hindsight (if only I'd known) 58
The Axe-man 59
Critics 61
Dorian Gray has a lot to answer for 62
Never put off till tomorrow 64
The Gypsy in us 66
The Wall 68

Thoughts about our dogs ! 71

For Max 72
That's not a dog it's a horse 74

Thoughts about when a life ends 77

I'm So Sorry For Your Loss 78
For Barry 79
The Space you left 80
Life's great game 82

Final Thoughts 85

My Passion 87

For Sue and Victoria
Without whose constant bullying these scribblings would never have seen the light of day

Preface

I have always written rhymes for as far back as I can remember. I don't know why, but it just felt right. Writing in rhyme somehow helps me to clarify and order my thoughts and occasionally entertain my friends and family.

I mostly write about things that impact my life, or that hurt me, provoke a reaction from me, or sometimes just make me feel that life is truly a wondrous adventure with an ever changing plot.

This is not a book of poetry, just a collection of my ramblings on a range of topics that happens to be written in rhyme.

People tell me that some of the things I write about are common to a lot of people, but it was never my intention to comment on other people's lives. What I write, is really just a series of personal thoughts about people, events and feelings in my own life, if they strike a chord with you then I am glad.

Just Trying to Make Sense of It All

I wish I was a poet

I am not a poet
I just write things down in rhyme
I write about things that happen
Whenever I have the time

I write about things that hurt me
As a way of getting by
I write about things that make me laugh
Or make me just feel high

But I wish I was a poet
Who could leave something behind
Like Byron Keats or Wordsworth
So someone else will find

The words that I have written
And just in some small way
Make them stop and think
That's how I felt today

Thoughts About Family Life
(Some good, some not so good)

Alan Spence

I tried to write to tell you

I tried to write to tell you
But the words just will not come
For once a line of simple rhyme
Is not easily done

I can't begin to put into words
The feelings that I feel
My world has finally come apart
Nothing seems quite real

The last few years have beaten me
And worn my strength away
I just don't have the energy
To fight another day

You've taken everything I have
And still come back for more
To rub more salt into the wounds
To make them still more raw

You think I judge you, but I don't
I just don't understand
Why you would wish to hurt me
Instead of hold my hand

Just Trying to Make Sense of It All

Inside I just feel hollow
I have nothing left to give
You've hurt me oh so many times
I've lost the will to live

So how long must I put up
With your selfish greedy ways
Why should it be, I don't believe
In anything you say

All I have now is the hope
That one day things will change
Because I love you very much
I know that must sound strange

But from the first day that I saw you
My heart was yours till the end of time
And however much you hurt me
You always will be mine

Alan Spence

Suddenly It Just Makes Sense

I sat and relaxed in the garden
On an April afternoon
The bright spring grass just sparkled
The blossom was starting to bloom

I watched as my beautiful daughter
Played with her beautiful boy
They laughed as they looked at the bushes
The spring leaves had just turned into toys

Jack plucked one and looked at me proudly
He had never picked a leaf before
And suddenly then it just struck me
That <u>this</u> is what life is for

To see them together and happy
Made my life seem so worthy and full
And everything else that I've strived for
Suddenly seemed quite dull

The love in their eyes shone so brightly
For each other, and also for me
As he toddled the length of the garden
With the leaf, just so that I could see

Just Trying to Make Sense of It All

It was just a leaf from a baby
But to me it was worth more than gold
A gift of priceless enlightenment
That could never be bought or sold

And in those few precious moments
My life just fell into place
The reason that I have existed
Shone in my grandsons face

Alan Spence

It's time that you both realised

It's time that you both realised
We have a life to live
We try to be good parents but,
There's only so much we can give

We need a little time for us
Our clock is ticking fast
We just don't know from day to day
How long our time will last

We love you both, but you are young
With all your life ahead
While we have so much left to do
Before we wake up dead

So just understand and don't be hurt
When we need some time alone
Please accept we need that time
Don't criticise or moan

Go out and organise your own lives
And live life to the full
Too soon you'll come to realise
The alternative is quite dull

Just Trying to Make Sense of It All

Because we need some time alone
Doesn't mean we love you less
But don't rely on us to come
And sort out all your mess

You're both grown up now
So act that way, manage your own life
And let us get on with ours
Free from dealing with your strife

We will always be your Mam and Dad
But please do not forget
We also are a man and wife
Not done with our lives yet

Alan Spence

I long to be close

I love my daughter dearly
More than words can say
I think about her often
Every single day

But I wish that she would understand
That when I disagree
With what she says, or what she does
It's just because I'm me

It doesn't mean I love her less
Or could ever love her more
But I can't agree, just to keep the peace
Or fight, just to even the score

I wish she knew that best advice
Is all I try to give
Some guidelines to help her through her life
To teach her how to live

To try to make her understand
About respect for all
But when I try to tell her
My words just hit a wall

Just Trying to Make Sense of It All

I guess I am not young enough
To be as wise as she
For she is always in the right
The wrong is left for me

I see it sometimes in her eyes
When she knows that I am right
But rather than admit it
She'd prefer to stand and fight

One day when she's older
I hope that she will see
The gulf that lies between us
Was not dug by me

I wish that I could bridge that gap
And that she could understand
Just how much I love her and
This distance was not planned

My words are only meant to help
Not drive us far apart
And although I know we are not close
There's no distance in my heart

Alan Spence

I need to make it right

There is dark where light should be
An empty hole inside of me
A void that can't be touched or seen
Where light not darkness should have been

I ask myself, what's not there
What is missing, why do I care
My life is good, but something's wrong
Some notes are missing from my song

I have a house, a job, a car
I can travel near and far
My larder is full, there's nothing I need
So what is this hunger I have to feed

I have a wife who loves me so
Who makes me happier than any could know
So how can I fill the empty hole
That still exists within my soul

I need to build a bridge between
The life I want and where I've been
Somewhere in the past I got it wrong
I lost the chorus to my song

Just Trying to Make Sense of It All

Without roots a tree will die
Without feathers a bird can't fly
So I need to see my children grow
I need this more than they could know

I guess this is my cross to bear
And they'll not realise, till I'm not there
Ever has it been the same,
But they need to know, they're not to blame

Whatever it was, they needed from me
I didn't give it, or they didn't see
Or they didn't want it, or they knew best
It's the same old story you can guess the rest

But then you get to a time in your life
When you don't want to argue, and can do without strife
So I hope against hope that the day will arrive
That we're a true family, While I'm still alive

When we stand alone we are easy to hurt
But standing together and wearing one shirt
We are strong, we are family, for all to see
Nothing else matters, it's how it should be

Alan Spence

Bad People

Sunday's come around again
And the family's come to call
Son and daughter with their kids
It's good to see them all

We love to cook the Sunday lunch
And do the washing up
While they bless us with their presence
And don't even wash a cup

We love that they, drink all our drink
And eat up all our food
While their babies cries, could split the skies
And tears rain down in floods

They think we should appreciate
When they come back to the nest
To thrust themselves upon us
And give themselves a rest

Other parents *"love it"*
That is what they say
So why do <u>we </u>not love it
Why do we dread the day

Perhaps we're just bad people
For feeling like we do
Perhaps we are just selfish
To have this point of view

Just Trying to Make Sense of It All

We do not want to hurt them
But we wish they'd understand
That we also have a life to live
And don't like it to be planned

Not even by our children
Or anyone else we know
We like to make our own plans
That's how it is and so . . . .

We're just not doting grandparents
I'm sorry but it's true
We still have places left to go
and many things to do

We love our family very much
But they must understand
Variety is the spice of life
And our life tastes quite bland

Doing the same thing every week
On the same old day
Cooking lunch and cleaning up
While they get in the way

We know that there is more to life
We just need time to play
So next weekend, when they come round
We'll be out for the day ☺

Alan Spence

Thank heavens for little girls . . . .
They grow up in the most delightful way—Maurice Chevalier

Those hateful spiteful teenage years
Have vanished into the past
The butterfly I knew was there
Has hatched and flown at last

It's hard to believe that such a change
Could happen in such a short time
And the daughter that I thought I'd lost
Would come back to be mine

The daughter that I longed for
Has been here all the while
The anger and the frowns have gone
Instead there is a smile

She is generous and sensitive
And brightens up my days
She makes me smile on the inside
With her loving caring ways

Just Trying to Make Sense of It All

No longer do I feel the need
To shout to lay down the law
I may have lost some battles
But I think I won the war

Those teenage memories quickly fade
As the years go rushing by
I'm just so glad that I lived to see
My beautiful butterfly

For Victoria

Alan Spence

The Parents Lament

Little do they know
The stress they put us through
With the little things they say
Or the little things they do

They never seem to realise
The impact of their deeds
They only ever stop to think
Of their own wants and needs

They wear the armour of their age
It keeps them safe from harm
The absolute wisdom of their youth
Acts like a magic charm

They forge ahead and live their life
Mistakes are left behind
They never see the consequence
They act as though they're blind

But one day revelation comes
It stops them in their tracks
It comes to us all at some stage
To change the way we act

For some they have a child of their own
For others it's just old age
But with advancing years comes wisdom
To make us all a sage

Just Trying to Make Sense of It All

"If only I'd known when I was young"
That's what we come to say
Then I would have done it differently
I would have changed my ways

At last they start to realise
That we knew what it was about
And that we also had the worry
Of how to sort it out

They slowly start to understand
That actions cause effects
That decisions have implications
And that <u>their</u> lives could be wrecked

They say you have to pay to learn
And mistakes are the price you pay
To buy your life experience
That guides you on your way

But its parents who usually foot the bill
With no chance of recompense
It's because we paid for their mistakes
That we have the common sense

So . . . .
The only solace I can give
As they put you through this hell
Is one day <u>they'll</u> be parents
And they'll suffer it as well !

Alan Spence

Responsibility

When our children are small they need great care
They need their parents to be there
To dry their tears and guide them through
Till they become an adult too

Till they can make their own life choices
And fight their corner with their own voices
To learn to stand alone and proud
To look for the silver that lies in each cloud

So why when they are fully grown
Do they come home to whinge and moan
Don't they know when they fly the nest
They should manage their own lives and just do their best

The same as their parents always have done
Life has its problems it's not always fun
But it seems that these days they're never to blame
They're not responsible, it's always the same

What should I do ? Please sort it out
It's not my fault we hear them shout
Why don't they realise the mess in their life
Is due to their actions that caused all this strife

Just Trying to Make Sense of It All

Well we've had enough now, we've done our fair share
We will still always love them and still always care
But their daily detritus is not ours to remove
Now <u>they</u> should stand up, Now <u>they</u> should prove

That being an adult is not about years
It's about facing your problems and confronting your fears
Overcoming your challenges in a positive way
I just hope that we'll live to see it some-day !

Alan Spence

When is it our turn

They want it all
They want it now
They have to have it
They don't care how
Hard work and time
Aren't part of their game
If they've no jam today
It's us that's to blame

When is it our turn
To enjoy what we've done
To savour the things
That our labours have won
Without feeling guilty
Without feeling wrong
For taking the time
To sing our own song

Always we've tried
To give them our best
We are the ones
Who have worked without rest
We are the ones
Who don't sleep at night
While they are out playing
Until it gets light

Just Trying to Make Sense of It All

When is it our turn
To feel that we've won
To feel that our job
Has at last been well done
When is it our turn
Do we ask too much
For a call or a note
To just stay in touch

When will the phone ring
And it not be a call
To give us their problems
For us to solve all
We always expected
To support them through life
But when is it our turn
To be free of their strife.

Alan Spence

Where are you Jack ?

A watched kettle never boils
That's what people say
And we've been watching ours now
For days and days and days
The bump is getting bigger
And it's really quite a size
Surely he should come out soon
To see the nice blue skies
We're getting a bit impatient now
It's gone beyond a joke
No little Jack to welcome
Not even waters broke !
If he doesn't come out soon
I don't know what we'll do
Perhaps we all should tell him
To come out and see the view
We could tempt him with some tasty treat
Or something nice to drink
Or threaten him if he doesn't come out
That we'll dress him up in pink
So please Jack if you're listening
Just come out and say hello
Just get yourself into the world
And make our faces glow !!

Just Trying to Make Sense of It All

Growing Pains !

I'm feeling sad, when I should be proud
While I watch him as he grows
I heave a sigh at what will come
Believe me, a mother knows

My little man who depends on me
For just about everything
Will soon move onward with his life
That's what the future brings

No more cosy home days in
While the rain pours down outside
Far less time for just us two
To sing and play and hide

Other people they will come
To change his loving ways
I've always known he would grow up
But I wish that he could stay

As my little man, my darling boy
The centre of my life
I desperately want to keep him
Safe from harm and safe from strife

Alan Spence

But he'll go to school, he'll make new friends
Find lots more things to do
He'll become more self sufficient
And develop his own views

I know that this will happen
And I wouldn't change it if I could
He needs to grow and find himself
I know this to be good

But part of me will keep him
In my heart, as my little boy
And the sadness I feel as I watch him grow
I know will turn to joy.

What is wrong with the world?

Alan Spence

Same World Different Rules

I heard a child cry bitterly
Because McDonalds was closed
Another child just sat and stared
Because no water flowed

The first child will move on with life
Despite his row and fuss
The second child will not be here
To sit and talk with us

There is no difference between them
They are both just the same
Just two small boys beginning their lives
Free from guilt or blame

One is not a wise child
Or the other one a fool
All that makes them different
Is same world different rules

Who you are and where you're born
Is just a thing of chance
In Africa or Scotland
In England or in France

Life is just a lottery
But the stakes are often high
Just the place that you are born
Can be why you live, or die

Just Trying to Make Sense of It All

Or if you get an education
Or don't even have a school
It's just a matter of location
Same world different rules

Some have everything they want
Not just everything they need
Their life's not ruled by choices
It's only ruled by greed

Some don't have any food to eat
Or clothes to keep them warm
Or a simple roof above their head
To shelter from the storm

So let me prick OUR conscience
And ask why we all don't give
It should not be that you could die
Just because of where you live.

So why should some have NOTHING
While others buy expensive jewels
We should be in this together
Not same world different rules

Alan Spence

Just be happy

I've always thought that people
Are wonderful and strange
But what is it with them these days
That makes them want to rearrange
The things that are unique to them
That make them who they are
Just to wear some smaller clothes
Or fill a bigger bra
Why do they all aspire
To turn into a clone
When they're already beautiful
Right down to the bone
The world would be a sadder place
If we all looked just the same
So why, oh why, do they do it
I wonder what's to blame
The things that makes us who we are
Come from deep within
So why this preoccupation
With the shape under your skin
So what! if you're slender as rake
Or curvy as ball
If you are happy with yourself
It doesn't matter at all
Changing who you really are
Shouldn't make you swell with pride
It's usually an original box
That holds the greatest treasures inside

Just Trying to Make Sense of It All

What's it all about

Please can you tell me
What is it all for
Keeping up with the Jones's
Being better than next door

Designer this, designer that
The label is the thing
But when it comes right down to it
What joy does it bring

It really doesn't matter
Where you live, or what you wear
But the world is now caught up in it
To the point I just don't care

To have the right accessories
To own the latest thing
Is all that matters these days
To make our sad hearts sing

What happened to the pleasure
Of just living for livings sake
Without greed or envy
Without the need to take

Alan Spence

Years ago we had much less
But felt that we had more
We shared the little that we had
We kept an open door

But times have changed
And no-one cares
They just take what they need
Forget about the caring, concentrate on greed

Why should I not have it?
Don't you know that I have rights?
They spit this venom easily
From their lowly heights

Today we have a culture
Of reward before the work
"We should all be equal"
The great unwashed all squawk

If they have it, then I want it
I'm just not prepared to work
I just left the school of life
With an NVQ in shirk

Just Trying to Make Sense of It All

Where is community spirit
When everyone cared for all
When you always held your hand out
If someone else did fall

Those days are far behind us now
Never to return
The book of help thy neighbour
Was set on fire and burned

Maybe I've had the best of times
And the worst is yet to be
I try to be an optimist
But it seems quite bad to me

I wish the clock would just turn back
To when I was a child
When the world was warm and fuzzy
Not greedy, hard and wild

Seasonal Thoughts

Alan Spence

A Christmas Thought

I can't believe that it's a year
Since the last time that we spoke
We promised that we'd stay in touch
But that's become a joke
The days pass by and then it's months
And soon a full year's gone
And how often have we spoken?
I think you'll find it's none.

So why does it take Christmas
To prompt a caring word,
Or the phone to ring, and a voice to say
"It's so long since we've heard . . . ."
From you, or Tom or Harry or Dick
You can fill in the name
The answer is that time's just flown
It's always been the same.

So let's give thanks for Christmas
Because then we take the time
To send a card, or make a call
Or write a little rhyme
And then we all remember
All the good times past
It's only because we're lazy
That we didn't make them last

Just Trying to Make Sense of It All

It's really not so difficult
To keep a friendship strong
To make that call, or send that note
It doesn't take too long
Life can pass us by so fast
And only when it ends
We find that how we've lived it
Is measured by our friends

So please let's try to keep in touch
More than once a year
There are other times than Christmas
When we should spread good cheer
Our friendship has not dimmed with time
I know it is still strong
I'd love to see you once again
I hope it won't be long

Alan Spence

Happy New Year

New Year's here
What's it about
Should I stay in
Should I go out
Am I just older
Am I a bore
Should I go out and party
Or just lock the front door
Should I stay in
And watch the TV
I just don't know
What's gotten into me
Once I was hungry
For excitement and fun
Now I don't feel that
Are my days all done?
I wish I could feel
Once again how I felt
When I was younger
When I was svelte
But try as I might
And do as I may
For me New Year's Eve
Is now just one more day

. . . . Sadly

Just Trying to Make Sense of It All

So this is Christmas

Christmas comes but once a year
Thank god for that, some will cheer
For some the season of good will
Turns out to be a bitter pill

For Christmas is the time of year
That far too often turns to tears
Instead of joy and peace for all
Family rifts come home to call

It seems to me the yuletide season
Often ends up as the reason
Why old issues come to the fore
And angst, not joy comes to the door

Hidden feelings and jealousy
Rear their head for all to see
Things not said throughout the year
Are now discussed loud and clear

Shouts and anger raise the roof
As if to offer some failed proof
That we were right and they were wrong
That this has gone on far too long

Alan Spence

That things now need to be laid to rest
That family loyalty's should be put to the test
Who sides with who, who was right
The arguments rail all through the night

I've been there and seen it, so I should know
That when it's over, all that shows
Are more fresh scars from battles old
A hollow feeling, a heart that's cold

Christmas fights do nothing more
Than salt old wounds and make them raw
Nothing is solved, nothing is gained
Rifts only deepen, bringing more pain

So take a hint from the festive season
Take the time to find a reason
To break with habit and make a change
Even if at first it's strange

The feeling that comes from just forgiving
Suddenly makes life worth living
Your empty heart's no longer hollow
And happiness is swift to follow

Just Trying to Make Sense of It All

So take a hint from one who knows
Take the chance just to show
That despite all that has gone before
Wounds can heal and not be sore

That blood is thicker than H_2O
That Christmas can restore the glow
It warms the heart and fills the space
It drives out bitterness and in its place.

Comes family bonds and love and care,
The feelings that were always there,
They just got lost along the way
So bring them back on Christmas Day

Some thoughts for people I know

Alan Spence

A Rhyme For No Reason

Sometimes things just happen
There is no-one to blame
Your life just changes forever
Never to be the same

Self-doubt and second guessing
Become your only friend
The quest to find an answer
Goes on without end

In your need to find an answer
You leave no stone unturned
There has to be a reason
Why you have been spurned

But rainbows come to see us
Only in the sun
Then they have to leave us
When their work is done

Just Trying to Make Sense of It All

The smile they leave upon our face
Was the reason they were here
The price they paid for the joy they brought
Costs us very dear

There is no rhyme or reason
Why things happen as they do
Know only that life's changes
Have nothing to do with you

So never stop believing
In what you know to be true
Just look to the sky for rainbows
And they will come to you

Alan Spence

The Magic Man

I have a friend called Barry
He is a magic man
If you want it and can't find it
My friend Barry can

It doesn't matter what you want
You've just to say the word
Before the sound has left your lips
My Friend Barry's heard

The next day bright and early
He'll turn up at your door
With a dozen lively lobsters
Or a leg of best wild boar

Or if you're looking for something special
And can't find anything that will do
Bazz will turn up at your door
With a choice of two

So be careful what you wish for
When my friend Barry's around
He'll find it before you know it
And charge you just a pound

It doesn't matter what you need
He'll get one the next day
He'll relieve you of your money
And then be on his way

Just Trying to Make Sense of It All

From a bar of whole-nut chocolate
To a giant fairground stand
A gallon can of tartan paint
Or a fifty piece brass band

Whatever you want he's got it
Or can get it the next day
Just let him know what it is you want
You only have to say

Some say he has a warehouse
Somewhere that no-one knows
A place where he keeps all his stock
So full it overflows

It's there so when you ask him
If he can help you out
He'll turn up trumps the very next day
Of that I have no doubt

From shiny pins to elephants
He has them all in there
He'll always get you what you want
Just because he cares

I haven't seen him for a while
But I've heard him laugh out loud
From just beyond the pearly gates
I bet he's selling clouds

Alan Spence

It's Not You

It's easy to sit alone and think
That things will never be the same
To feel that it is all your fault
And that it's you to blame

But don't be swayed by those around
Who are always quick to judge
Who find it easy to criticise
And hold a lasting grudge

Don't be hurt by thoughtless words
Or silence without end
You cannot pick your family
So just listen to your friends

It's not your job to take the blame
For things that others have done
And if you do, and blame yourself
It's the others who have won

Believe that you have done your best
When you know this to be true
Sometimes things just happen
That have nothing to do with you

Just Trying to Make Sense of It All

It's always easier to point and blame
Than to understand and care
But it's the right of the small of mind
To look down with a withering glare

So never doubt just who you are
And <u>know</u> that you are right
Never forget that the brightest days
Follow the darkest nights

Alan Spence

Mistakes don't matter

Growing up I've made mistakes
I've not had many lucky breaks
Some look at me with a condemning stare
I want them to know that I just don't care

My life is mine to live as I choose
Sometimes I win sometimes I lose
Sometimes I bend but I will not break
I just carry on for my children's sake

I want you to know when you look in my eye
My two little girls are the stars in my sky
They make me so proud as I watch them play
They give me the reason to get through each day

The joy that they bring is worth all the pain
They are my sunshine after the rain
Though some of my life has been quite a mess
When I look at my girls I feel truly blessed

So please do not judge me as different from you
Each of us has our own point of view
I just try to be the best I can be
If you cannot see it you're just different to me

Just Trying to Make Sense of It All

You don't know what you've got till it's gone

I went to see a friend today
To talk about old times
To once again share memories
Stored in our common mind
But the friend I knew was out today
When I came to call
Instead a stranger sat there
Staring at the wall
I asked him where my friend had gone
He said he didn't know
He said he didn't know me
He said that I should go
He didn't mean to hurt me
But a tear ran down my cheek
Because my friend was sitting there
Only just last week
How can it be
My lifelong friend
Doesn't even know my face
How can he look right past me
Into empty space
What a cruel thief this life can be
To take memories so dear
But I will come again next week
I hope my old friends here.

Thoughts about life in general

Alan Spence

Things to be happy about
(A homage to "Reasons to be cheerful")

Waking up in the morning
A new day dawning
A soft breeze or the sun on your face
An act that is kind
Or love that is blind
The thought of your favourite place

The sight of a rainbow
The soft light of moon glow
Through clouds in a dark frosty sky
A child full of glee
Fish and chips by the sea
The thought of a real bargain buy

The smell of a new car
A pint in a great bar
The smell of some wholesome hot food
A pocket full of money
A sight that is funny
Or something a little bit rude

Your dog coming to meet you
A friends shout to greet you
Knowing things have worked out just fine
A weekend away
A hot summers day
Some cheese with a glass of fine wine

Just Trying to Make Sense of It All

Just feeling healthy
Or a little bit wealthy
Or having nothing to worry about
A hug from your mother
Or a kiss from your lover
And not ever suffering from gout

This list is endless
And unless you're friendless
You should be happy for most of the time
Fill your time with pleasure
As if each day's a treasure
And I'm sure life will treat you just fine !

Alan Spence

Choices

Don't tell people your troubles
They're not bothered if you're sad
Most of them don't give a hoot
And the rest of them are glad

Don't think that you're a victim
When things don't go your way
Just take what comes right on the chin
And start afresh next day

Your life is yours for you to live
So live it best you can
The way you face life's challenges
Is the measure of the man

The path of life has many roads
And no-one knows the way
So it comes down to the choices we make
Each and every day

So live by your decisions
Whether right or wrong
Move onward and move upward
Live life well, and live it long

Learn by each mistake you make
Get smarter every day
This is <u>your</u> life so enjoy it
There is no other way.

Just Trying to Make Sense of It All

Tempus Fugit

The clock is always ticking
It gets faster by the day
Everybody feels it
Perhaps that is why they say
Time flies or tempus fugit
They both mean just the same
The days just pass by faster
There is no-one to blame

When I was just a little lad
A day seemed like a week
Now a days more like an hour
Almost over as we speak
No time to smell the flowers
As we rush past our in haste
We should savour every second
We have no time to waste

How does time pass faster
Than it did when I was small
When the summer stayed forever
And there was time enough for all
Why is it that as you grow old
Time passes in a blink
I wish I knew the answer
It really makes you think

Alan Spence

Go back if you need to

The path of life is twisty
It can be a bumpy track
To find your way going forward
Sometimes you must go back

It doesn't mean you're cowardly
Or lack a well thought plan
It just means it's sometimes best
To go back if you can

There is more to life than property
Or the accumulation of great wealth
Take time to think of happiness
Your family and your health

The days pass by so quickly
So please don't waste your time
Putting up and making do
Instead of feeling fine

So if along life's journey
You wander off the track
Please don't sit and worry
Because you can go back

Admitting you have made mistakes
Doesn't make you less
Just look again at your life plan
And sort out all the mess

Just Trying to Make Sense of It All

Move forward if you need to
To find a better place
Or sort it out right where you are
If that is what it takes

But don't forget you could go back
To where you used to be
And if you will be happy there
Take this advice from me

Life's too short to spend your days
Struggling with yourself
It will affect your family
It will affect your health

Find what it is you love to do
And do it every day
And if you do it for a living
Then work will seem like play

Better to be a happy man
With a smile upon your face
Than spend your life just worrying
Like most of the human race.

Alan Spence

Hindsight (if only I'd known)

Hindsight is a wonderful thing
It opens up our eyes
With the benefit of hindsight
We all are very wise

If we could only know the outcome
Before we made the choice
How very much more confident
Would become our voice

But hindsight only happens
When the die is cast
Only when the outcome's known
Does hindsight come at last

So sadly we must live our lives
Taking our best guess
Just hoping that we get it right
And not end up in a mess

Just Trying to Make Sense of It All

The Axe-man

Sad to say todays the day
The axe-man came to call
I lost my job out of the blue
My life went into stall

A takeover was the problem here
Big business was to blame
Growth and profit makes the rules
It really is a shame

The human cost is usually more
Than the price the business paid
Your life goes into turmoil
Your best laid plans unmade

But then I thought just catch your breath
Take stock of who you are
Take control of your destiny
Don't let job loss be a bar

Your life is still your own to live
They can't take that away
Just get yourself back on your feet
To fight another day

To come, could be the best of times
More than went before
Don't look ahead and see a wall
Look through an open door

Alan Spence

To pastures new and views beyond
Where bright new treasures lie
Just look past the storm clouds
For the sunshine in the sky

We are not in this world for long
So just give it your best shot
Don't ever think you've had your day
Believe me you have not

Life is full of twists and turns
This is just another bend
You've just lost your wage for now
Not your family and friends

So even though things may look bleak
Don't let it get you down
Tomorrow is a bright new day
Don't greet it with a frown

Opportunities and challenges
Are always there to find
The only thing that stops you
Is usually in your mind

Nil illegitimi carborundum

Just Trying to Make Sense of It All

Critics

A critic's just a person with a point of view
You mostly only like them
If they agree with you
Some may be quite expert
On the topic of their choice
Others do it just because
They like the sound of their own voice
What they say is just opinion
It's definitely not a fact
Just take it with a pinch of salt
And don't ever over react
Do not base your judgements
On what someone else has said
Better to investigate and
Find out yourself instead.

Alan Spence

Dorian Gray has a lot to answer for

I suppose I'm getting older
But I still feel just the same
In my head I am still thirty
In my heart there burns a flame

But lately I've begun to notice
Things aren't how they used to be
Why is the print getting smaller
So small I cannot see

Why have they gone and changed it
It used to be just right
And now I have to read it
Under a bright white light

Why are things much heavier
Than just a few years ago
Why does everything that I do
Seem to be so slow

Why do I feel compelled to groan
When I bend down to the floor
Why do I just walk up the stairs
And not run up anymore

Why do I go to get something
And when I get there I've forgot
What it was I went there for
My memory's just shot

Just Trying to Make Sense of It All

I used to make decisions
And make my mind up in a blink
Now the simplest basic task
Makes me stop and think

And by the time I've decided
What it is I was going to do
I have to put it off a while
To nip off to the loo

Why is alcohol stronger
Than it used to be
Only a couple of drinks these days
Is more than enough for me

My appetite has dwindled
Although my waist has grown
And instead of telling lots of jokes
All I do is moan . . .

About the troubles in the world
About our wayward youth
Suddenly the penny drops
And I realise the truth

I am not thirty anymore
And I'm starting to feel sad
The vibrant Adonis I used to be
Has turned into my Dad

Alan Spence

Never put off till tomorrow

Never put off till tomorrow
What you can do today
You hear it time and time again
That's what people say

But how many of us do that
And do things right away
Not that many I would guess
It gets done the next day

We think we are immortal
And have time enough to spare
We treat each precious glorious day
As if we just don't care

But think how different things would be
If we could only know
Just how much time was left for us
Before we have to go

A day, a week, a month, a year,
The answers still the same
There never would be enough time left
To finish playing our game

Just Trying to Make Sense of It All

So let me give you some advice
To speed you on your way
Life's for living, so do it now
Don't put off one more day

Don't make plans for the future
For you know not what it holds
You never know when it will end
As your life unfolds

So don't just <u>wish</u> to do things
<u>Make</u> your dreams come true
The only thing that stops you
Is mostly always you

You can't take it with you
Is truer than you know
It's no good wishing you'd done things
When it's time for you to go

So fulfil all your ambitions
Treat each day like a race
Because when the race is over
You'll just be dust in space

Alan Spence

The Gypsy in us

I really do like living here
No traffic noise
The air is clear
No litter lies about the place
No yobs to shout into your face
The sound of water running by
The stars that blink in a dark night sky
A place to live without being seen
A garden soft and warm and green
Where friends can come
And stay a while
A place that simply makes me smile

But living here I've come to know
The time has come for us to go
Not because of anything here
Let me make that very clear
It's just there's more to life than this
Our friends and family are a miss
A quick trip out down to the shops
A social life that never stops
Lots to see and lots to do
So off again to pastures new
That's not to say we won't go back
To where the pace of life is slack
"Never say never" is what we say
And sometime there may come a day

Just Trying to Make Sense of It All

When we'll go back and maybe stay
But that time is a while away
Still too many things to do
Just to sit and admire the view
The gypsy in us is still strong
So we're still looking for where we belong

Alan Spence

The Wall

I built a wall outside my fence
I thought no-one would see
But someone did and told a man
That's not where that wall should be

The man he looked and thought a bit
And then he said to me
You've built a wall that seems quite nice
But not where it should be

And so it was, and on it went
the issue of the wall
Sometimes I wish I'd never built
The bloody thing at all

I just can't see what harm it does
To build a wall just there
It really didn't bother ME
But someone seems to care

So now the wall may have to move
I'll have to wait and see
If I can leave my lovely wall
Right where it should not be

Just Trying to Make Sense of It All

The man will think it over
And then come back to me
He'll let me know if it can stay
Where it ought not to be

But if I have to move it
To start over once again
I guess I'll have to knock it down
What a bloody pain !

The Moral . . . .
To build a wall is wonderful
A lovely thing to see
But just be very careful
And build where it should be
Cos' if you don't I promise you,
And it's a guarantee
Some nosy git will shop you
Just you wait and see !

Thoughts about our dogs !

Alan Spence

For Max

There are times in your life if you're lucky
That something wonderful comes along
Sometimes it's a person
Sometimes a poem, or a song

But when it comes it will change you forever
You can never tell in what way
Sometimes for good, sometimes for ill
I'm afraid you never can say

It's of one of these times that I'm writing
We were luckier than we could have known
We thought we'd just bought a little white dog
To give him a safe happy home

But I cannot begin to tell you
Because I don't have the words to say
The joy that Max has given us
From the start of that very first day

He been faithful and loyal and funny
Though he's always done his own thing
We did not know when we got him
The fun and the love he would bring

Just Trying to Make Sense of It All

For inside that small fluffy body
Beat the heart of a hero of old
There was nought in this world that could scare him
He was steadfast courageous and bold

But now he's no longer with us
He has gone to where all good dogs go
He was a friend that was truer than any
We miss him more, than you ever could know.

Alan Spence

That's not a dog it's a horse

When you own an Irish Wolfhound
Many things must change
You need to get a bigger car
The house needs re-arranged
But one thing I did not expect
And it came as a shock to me
Is that I suddenly changed from anonymous
Into an A list celebrity

For when walking with a Wolfhound
You really do stand out
So get ready for the photographs
Get ready for the shouts
"It's a horse" you hear them cry
As everyone stops to stare
How much does he eat?
You must have a big house?
"That's not a dog . . . . it's a bear"

So perhaps you need a tee shirt
With the answers on the back
But that would only spoil the fun
And take away the craic
So revel in your new found fame
While the limelight you can hog
But before your head swells up too big
Remember, it's for the dog

Just Trying to Make Sense of It All

You'll hear these things wherever you go
And whenever you go out
It could really start to wear quite thin
If you forgot what it's all about
For the wonder and the pleasure
That Wolfhounds do bestow
On everyone who meets them
Just makes their faces glow

You will realise quite early on
How privileged you are
To share your life with one so proud
Underwhelmed at being a star
Totally aloof when all around
Are stunned by what they see
So I stand with pride next to his side
While no-one looks at me

So . . . . the thing that I did not expect
Is the last thing I would change
To have a Wolfhound in your life
Is wonderful and strange
So I treat my role as second best
To a giant hairy hound
As a treasure beyond my wildest dreams
I wouldn't trade, for a million pounds

For Harry

Thoughts about when a life ends

Alan Spence

I'm So Sorry For Your Loss

I wish that I could make it right
And turn your darkness into light
Remove your hurt, remove your pain
Remove the anger and the blame

I never meant to just dismiss
The loss you feel for the one you miss
My words weren't meant to hurt you so
Only to help you, to let go

To help you know that life goes on
Even though the pains not gone
And to be with you as you come to know
That the pain will never really go

To wait with you until you accept
That the loss you feel and the tears you've wept
Will hurt you less, though they'll still remain
Till you can bear your sorrow, and accept your pain

The day will come, of this I'm sure
When you'll be able to endure
I cannot say when it will be
And it won't be because of me
For try as I might and long as I may
I cannot take your pain away

So please don't blame or be angry with me
Just because I cannot see
The way to make things right again
Because I can never heal your pain.

Just Trying to Make Sense of It All

For Barry

Sometimes when I sit in the warm sunshine
Eating good food or drinking fine wine
My thoughts will stray to a friend that I know
He should still be here, but he had to go

I know that he would rather have stayed
There were stories to tell and games to be played
Deeds to be done and fun to be had
Things still to do, to make people glad

But sometimes life just ruins your plan
And how you react defines the man
The man that I speak of could never be cowed
And to call him my friend, still makes me feel proud

Better a life, lived hard, to the full
Than settling down to a life that is dull
"Better to burn out than rust out" he'd say
So that's what he did, that was his way

So please don't feel sad for a life full of joy
For a man in his autumn, who was still a boy
Who woke every morning and cherished each day
And who had to leave us, when we all hoped he'd stay

The Space you left

My life is full but there's a space
An empty void a lonely place
I have it all but the space remains
I cannot fill it except with pain

Each day I ask please tell me why
A part of me has had to die
No answer comes the pains still there
No one else even seems to care

Can they not see the hole in my heart
The jigsaw piece the missing part
Can they not feel the loss I do
Surely she was part of their life too

But they never felt her love for me
For if they had they all would see
The pain I feel is the price I pay
For the love she gave me every day
If others feel the pain less strong
Perhaps it's because they heard less of her song

Just Trying to Make Sense of It All

Her song stays with me every day
In all I do and all I say
Without the pain I'd forget her song
I'd still be weak not whole and strong

For though she's gone
She's still here with me
And that is how
It has to be

Always it has been the same
It cannot change
There is no blame
The greater the loss
The greater the pain
Now that she's gone
Just the space remains

Alan Spence

Life's great game

Don't mourn for me when I'm not here
Just go out and have a beer
Behave like things are just the same
And carry on with life's great game

Be thankful for the times we've had
Remember them and don't be sad
"Life goes on" is what I believe
So enjoy <u>your</u> turn and please don't grieve

Just because I've left the field
Doesn't mean that you can quit
You must play until the end
That's the truth of it

Play it hard and play it long
Each day give it your all
Remember while you're on the field
It's <u>your</u> turn on the ball

One fine day your game will end
There is no other way
Until that time give it all you've got
Go out and have your day

Just Trying to Make Sense of It All

Live each day as best you can
Like each day was your last
Live it large and live it long
For soon it will be past

All my life I've done my best
To live my life this way
To cherish every moment
And relish every day

To do as much as possible
To experience different things
To learn to face life's challenges
To enjoy the change they bring

The one truth I have truly learned
Is there's never enough time
So savour every second
Like a glass of vintage wine

I don't regret a moment
Of this precious life I've had
So please don't mourn my passing
I've enjoyed it, so be glad

Alan Spence

Celebrate the time I've had
Don't grieve because I'm gone
Remember that I truly believe
That life should just go on

We owe it to the ones we love
To tell them before we go
That their life goes on without us
And that they all should know

We want then to enjoy their life
Now that our time's past
So please don't sit and mourn for me
Go out and have a blast ☺

Final Thoughts

Just Trying to Make Sense of It All

My Passion

Sometimes I'm moved to sit and write
To change the grey to black and white
To clear the fog that fills my brain
Or just to help to keep me sane

For we all have within us
A yearning to express
To make order out of chaos
Or a balance to redress

We have emotions that can move us
to be more than we can be
to drive us ever onward
to see what we can see

or to chase a dream that haunts us
or achieve a lifelong goal
or just fill a void within us
that somehow makes us whole

a passion is within us all
it's part of who we are
for some it brings contentment
for others, wounds and scars

for me, I need to leave some words
to say I passed this way
before I return to dust of stars
I need to have my say

Printed in Great Britain
by Amazon.co.uk, Ltd.,
Marston Gate.